T5-CVH-961

CONTENTS

FOREWORD

SPACE OPERATIONS of the future should have one central objective: the addition of new environmental regimes to Man's domain, in order to assure the long-term survival of our terrestrial environment. In the century ahead, the two most important new regimes will be the orbital space of Earth and the surfaces of relatively readily accessible sister worlds — Moon, Mars, Mercury and certain asteroids. Man in space can add considerable value to space operations. He provides judgment and responsiveness. He furnishes on-the-spot scientific interpretation and improves the quality and usefulness of scientific instruments through greater control of what is being measured or observed and when. He makes possible a high degree of operational and mission flexibility not attainable with purely automated systems.

From orbital space—in cooperation with appropriate ground action—we can monitor and manage the resources and biosphere of our planet through atmospheric and surface measurements. Orbital information transmission stations can spread knowledge, skills and enlightenment to all mankind. Eventually we will manufacture new products in orbit and generate electric power in orbit to be beamed to Earth for consumption at a minimum of ecological interference. Space stations and lunar bases will become great new centers of scientific research, because these vantage points permit observations and experiments to be conducted that cannot be duplicated on Earth.

All these accomplishments can be realized in the first half of the next hundred years. With them will come the development of appropriate transportation systems, from Space Shuttle through interorbital shuttles to interplanetary ships. In the second half we will begin to exploit raw materials on other worlds, thus expanding mankind's industrial resources and living standard without adding to this planet's ecological burden. In spite of all progress, the future of Man faces grave new crises if he remains confined to one planet only. Earth and space must become indivisible for the sake of assuring mankind's continued ascendancy as well as the preservation of our environment. The surge into the unknown must go on, and with all deliberate speed. This book is a fine contribution to bringing our next steps into the unknown closer to the understanding of our youth in whose hands their successful achievement will lie.

DR. KRAFFT A. EHRICKE
Chief Scientific Advisor
Advanced Programs, Space Division
North American Rockwell

INTO THE UNKNOWN

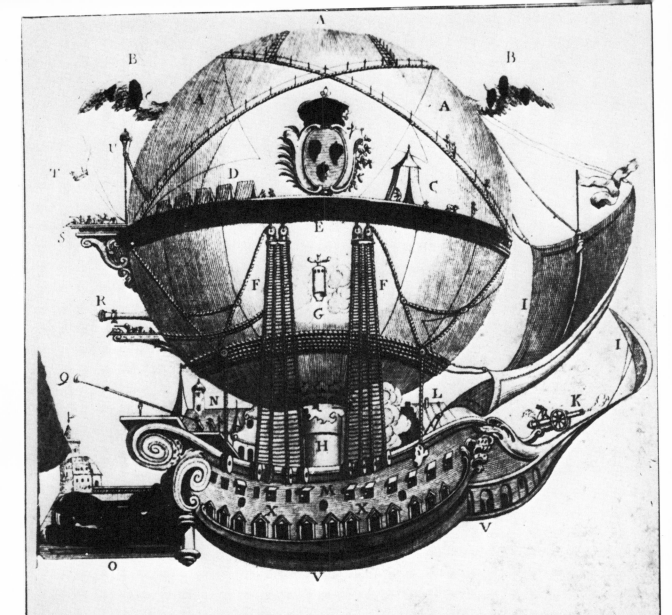

History's first "Space Station" was this 1784 visionary scheme for an orbiting military base to be manned by the French Army. By 1984 the United States plans to have scientific space stations in orbit for peaceful, not military, purposes.

INTO THE UNKNOWN

The Story of Space Shuttles

and Space Stations

By Don Dwiggins
Illustrated with Photographs and Diagrams

GOLDEN GATE JUNIOR BOOKS
SAN CARLOS • CALIFORNIA

*To the valiant men of the Air Force Flight Test Center
and NASA Flight Research Center,
who pioneered the way to space flight,
this book is respectfully dedicated.*

AUTHOR'S PREFACE

IN THE LONG history of human exploration it has remained for an adventurous few to leave the comforting certainties of their homes and go beyond the horizon, pushing back barriers of ignorance we call the unknown. However, few pioneers won recognition for their achievements. When Christopher Columbus reached America in 1492, already forgotten Basques and Norsemen had preceded him. And when Russia's first *Sputnik* orbited the earth in November, 1957, few remembered that the United States Air Force had, one month earlier, already rocketed objects into a solar orbit, from White Sands, New Mexico—man's first reach into the void of outer space.

Hindsight serves little purpose, other than to assess the direction and practicality of future explorations as we penetrate deeper into the solar system. Landing a man on the moon and returning him safely to earth was more than just America's space goal for the 1960's; that achievement stands as the beginning of an entirely new era of space exploration. Just as colonials came to America to settle the New World, once its frontiers had been opened, so will future space colonials one day extend man's habitat hundreds of miles upward. In this book, the author has tried to tell the story of where space exploration will take us, as well as how and where it all began. The link making possible man's migration into space is, of course, the remarkable Space Shuttle, destined to become the ultimate aerospacecraft, able to fly both inside the atmosphere and above it.

Hardware exists for America's first Experimental Space Station (XSS), called Skylab, and plans are on the drawing boards for future orbiting space colonies, where up to 100 people will live and work for months and years at a time. No longer the realm of science fiction, these breath-taking projects stand as new challenges to science and technology, widening man's horizons to encompass the distant planets, and at the same time making life on planet Earth better for all.

DON DWIGGINS

ACKNOWLEDGMENTS

THE AUTHOR is indebted to many individuals who gave their time to supply recollections of the early days of aerospace research flight and to blueprint the most probable future of our National Space Transportation System of space shuttles and space stations. Among them were Gus Briegleb, H. D. Froning, Jr., Bernhard A. Hohmann, Dr. George Mueller, Dr. Ludwig Roth, General Charles Yeager, and Dr. Fritz Zwicky.

Thanks also goes to the author's numerous friends in government and industry who made their files available and supplied information and photographs for this space book, the fifth title written by the author and published by Golden Gate Junior Books. Prime sources include Aerospace Corporation, Bell Aircraft Corporation, General Dynamics Convair Division, Grumman Aerospace Corporation, Hughes Aircraft Company, Martin Marietta Corporation, McDonnell Douglas Corporation, National Aeronautics and Space Administration's Ames and Langley Research Centers, NASA Edwards Flight Research Center, NASA Houston Manned Spacecraft Center and Kennedy Space Center, North American Rockwell Corporation, Northrop Corporation, Pan American World Airways, TRW, Inc., University of California at Los Angeles, and the United States Air Force's Edwards Flight Test Center, Aerospace Research Pilot School, Systems Command, and Vandenberg Air Force Base.

A RIDE ON TOMORROW'S SPACE SHUTTLE

THE DATE is July 20, 1979, and you have a funny feeling in your stomach as you walk toward Launch Complex 39 at Cape Kennedy.

You are a physical scientist, and you've never been in space before. You pause to stare up at the monstrous shuttle craft you are about to enter. Mated to its mammoth booster, it stands proudly against its gantry, 265 feet high—taller than the Statue of Liberty by more than 100 feet—a strange-looking aerospaceship, reminding you of a giant manta.

The thought crosses your mind—today is the tenth anniversary of the historic moment when man first set foot on the moon, when Astronaut Neil Armstrong's electric message flashed across 240,000 miles of space —"Eagle has landed!"

All that seems ages ago, for much has happened since Skylab, America's first experimental space station, early in this decade proved that men could live and work in orbit for months at a time with no ill effects. Since the launching of the first permanent, 12-man space station (we'll call it *Argus I*) following Skylab, a total of 48 scientists and engineers have ridden the shuttle plane as passengers, to work on special projects.

Up ahead, the other passengers on this trip are gathering at the gantry elevator, dressed in comfortable lint-free nylon coveralls and carrying light-weight suitcases. It looks for all the world like an ordinary airline terminal scene as they are checked off the passenger list, one by one.

There is a university professor whose specialty is X-ray astronomy ... a young doctor whose field is human organ transplants ... a pretty young lady ecologist involved in worldwide air pollution studies ... an Air Force colonel studying air defense expansion into space.

You check your watch—45 minutes to launch. Already the two craft have been loaded with 3,000,000 pounds of liquid oxygen and hydrogen fuel. The flight crew—captain and copilot—is seated in the cockpit of the orbiter. Another crew is in position in the booster's cockpit.

You ride the elevator up and cross a walkway to the orbiter, then descend the access ladder to your seat, third row, center aisle. You stow your briefcase and settle back into the comfortable contour couch, fasten seat belt and shoulder harness, and listen to piped country music over the loudspeaker.

The passenger cabin is roomy, and when the access door is closed and locked you have the feeling of being inside a conventional jetliner, except that it's sitting on its tail. You smile at the other passengers, most of whom you know. You'll be living with them in the same "space hotel" until you rocket back for the Christmas holidays.

Even though the flight time to rendezvous with *Argus I* will be about the same as in a subsonic transcontinental flight from New York to San Francisco, you notice a well-stocked galley and lavatory facilities — the shuttle is equipped for a seven-day stay in space should weather or other factors delay its return to earth.

Looking straight ahead, you watch the pilot and copilot go through their preflight checkout. The flight controls look much like those of the X-15 and the Apollo spacecraft, for maneuvering through orbital operations, reentry, and landing. Most of the instrument displays are automatic; in the center of the panel is a cathode-ray tube like a TV screen, on which the shuttle's actual flight path will be traced for comparison with the theoretical computed trajectory the pilot should be flying. The same display will show ground terrain and flight path information during reentry and landing.

You glance through a small brochure the flight attendant handed you on the gantry. It tells you that the booster and orbiter together weigh 5,000,000 pounds. The orbiter is the lightest, yet at 760,000 pounds it is as heavy as a fully loaded C5A Galaxy of the early 1970's. Twelve

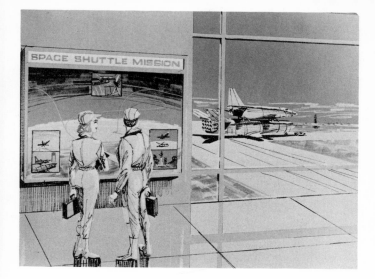

rockets in the booster each deliver 550,000 pounds of thrust—for a total of 6,600,000 pounds!

"Attention," the loudspeaker suddenly interrupts. "Flight one-oh-six ready for liftoff!"

Your hands clench in anticipation, then you glance at the pretty ecologist next to you and relax. There is a noticeable rumble, not much louder than that of a turbojet taking off, because of the soundproofing. The ecologist smiles reassuringly and points out the window.

You glance out and see large clouds of clear smoke billowing around you, coming from the rocket exhaust. The shuttle rises; in seven seconds you are clear of the launch tower—about half the time of an Apollo-Saturn V liftoff, because of the shuttle's higher initial thrust-to-weight ratio.

The acceleration continues as the shuttle bores through a light overcast and emerges, like salmon breaking water, into the bright sky above. You feel heavier now. Two minutes after liftoff your weight has tripled, but now the booster pilots are throttling their engines and things stay the same as the shuttle's flight path curves over toward the horizontal.

12

At three minutes into the flight the main booster engines shut down. Quietness fills the cabin, then suddenly the sound of the two orbiter engines starting up is heard. The orbiter separates from the booster, and as it climbs away you look back through the window and see the booster rolling and banking as it begins its return to the launch area. On the way down, the booster will maneuver through a 520-mile cruiseback, holding its gravity forces to 3.0, to keep 90 percent of its skin from exceeding 2000°F through air friction.

You notice the acceleration again building—to 3 g's as the orbiter flies

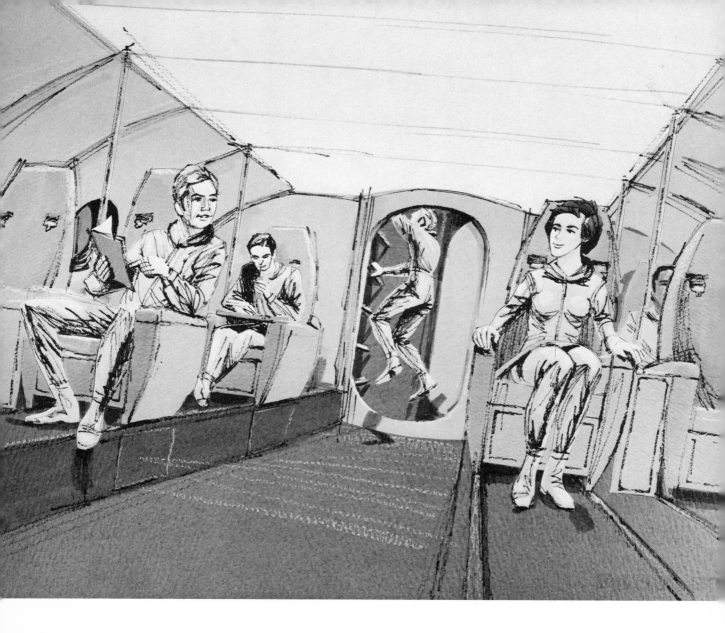

nearly parallel to the earth's surface. Four minutes after separation from the booster the orbiter's main engines shut down, 50 miles above the Atlantic Ocean and some 100 miles downrange from Kennedy Space Center.

Your arms float upward and you discover you are weightless! The orbiter is coasting uphill, to a 100-mile-high apogee, and you laugh and chat with the ecologist, who is amused by her pencil floating away through the cabin.

At an altitude of 100 miles the craft's on-orbit engines fire briefly, about 48 seconds, and the vehicle swings into a circular orbit. The "Fasten Seat

Belts" sign goes off, and presently you are enjoying floating about the cabin. You find the ecologist's pencil and swim back toward her with it, then strap yourself down once more as the pilots unstrap their star trackers and sextants, obtain precise spatial fixes, and feed the information into an onboard computer. Quickly the computer calculates the proper thrust-level, burn time, and thrust direction for maneuvering the orbiter toward the space station.

This exciting "space chase" takes a minimum of one hour, during which time the orbiter again fires its rockets to climb to the 240-mile orbit where

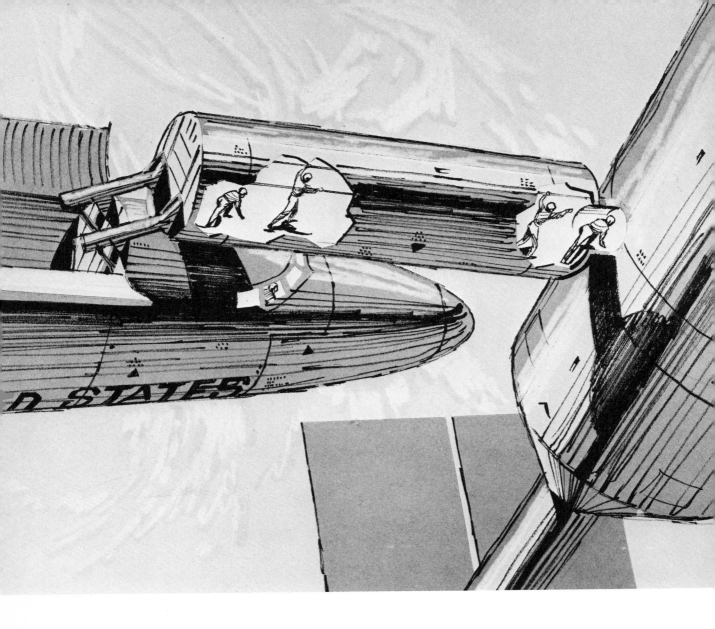

Argus I is flying. The captain calls an observer in the space station.

"Roger," the observer radios back. "We have you on radar and laser link."*

Smoothly the orbiter is guided into docking position. Its cargo doors swing open and a cylindrical cargo container rotates out and to the front, at the end of a mechanical arm. Carefully the shuttle pilot and the space station observer bring the two craft together, until the docking mechanism, a part of the cargo container, locks into place.

*Lasers, meaning *l*ight *a*mplification by *s*timulated *e*mission of *r*adiation, provide highly accurate distance measurement, were first used in space to pinpoint Apollo 11's landing site on the moon.

The container is pressurized by the space station attendant and you hear the hiss of air as an airlock is opened. You can now float up through the passageway into the space station without donning a bulky pressure suit.

Inside the space station, you shake hands with the departing 12-man crew which you and your fellow passengers are replacing, and you wish each one a good trip back to earth. Then you go to your quarters, stow your gear, and look over the snug satellite that will be your home for the next six months.

Like the other passengers, you have been trained in several disciplines

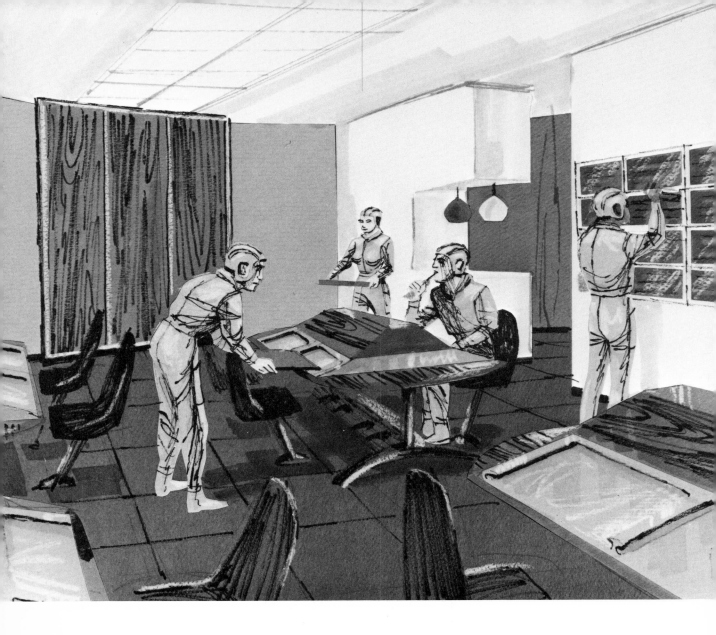

—radio astronomy, biology, geology, nuclear physics — for you will be working side by side with brilliant scientists at a variety of exciting tasks.

Now, for the first time, you and your crewmates are able to monitor the earth's dwindling store of natural resources on a totally global scale. You study water pollution in all the oceans, rivers, and lakes of the world, and, with multispectral photography, chart a wide range of things—from hidden mineral deposits to blighted forests.

Training your radio telescope on distant galaxies, unhampered by atmospheric distortion, you look backward through time, across billions

of light years, to study the universe as it existed at the time of creation.

In December your tour of duty is over. You prepare to depart on the next shuttle for Cape Kennedy, anxious to be with friends and relatives again. You have already seen a mantle of snow blanketing Canada and the northern United States and your thoughts have turned to Christmas.

You watch the shuttle that will take you home move into view, and you feel the slight jar as it docks with the space station. You greet the new replacement crew as a veteran spaceman, and soon you're aboard and in your seat for the return journey. The shuttle drifts away under the

nudging of small jet thrusters which turn the orbiter around so that it flies backward. The main rockets fire and you sink back into the contour couch as the de-orbit phase of the flight begins.

The shuttle streaks across the top of the world, along a curving flight path that brings you down across Alaska, Canada, and the Pacific Northwest. Flying through its transition maneuver, the craft enters the atmosphere in a nose-high attitude, and the pilots begin to kill off speed in a series of high cross-range turns.

Unlike a returning Apollo capsule, the space shuttle capsule has sufficient

maneuverability to land, in an emergency, in any of the 48 contiguous
states having a 10,000-foot runway, but on this flight the weather is clear
and all systems *go* for Cape Kennedy.

Looking out the window, you can see a storm system moving across the
western states, bringing snow to the Rockies. Finally, you see the Florida
peninsula down below as the pilot banks the orbiter over steeply.

"Prepare for landing," his voice instructs on intercom.

You settle back in your contour seat, just like any ordinary airline passenger, feeling the deceleration as the pilot opens his dive brakes and lines

up on final approach at airliner speed. Two fanjet engines emerge from the fuselage—and there is the familiar whine as the shuttle crosses the end of the field and touches down at an easy 173 knots.

You're back on earth again, after six months in a weightless state, and the grip of gravity feels good. Still better, you'll be home for Christmas!

This imaginative journey aboard a space shuttle of the late 1970's is more fact than fiction, for it is based on actual National Aeronautics and Space Administration plans for a National Space Transportation System to follow the highly successful Apollo program. The next chapter tells the little-known story of how this program began a quarter of a century ago.

TO THE EDGE OF SPACE

Bell XS-1 was world's first supersonic aircraft.

A STARTLING explosion shook the peace and quiet of the Antelope Valley region of California's Mojave Desert early on the crisp fall morning of October 14, 1947. Ranchers paused at their work to look around, perplexed. Rabbits scurried into their holes and wheeling hawks folded their wings to dive for cover.

The sound came from high above, where the white vapor trail of a streaking rocket ship from nearby Muroc Dry Lake drew a thin pencil line across the sky, like a speeding arrow. It was history's first sonic boom, the sound of the future. With that man-made thunderclap, the United States in effect announced that it was on its way into space. Riding the point of the shock wave at 760 miles per hour, Air Force Captain Charles E. Yeager had broken the sound barrier in the Bell research craft XS-1—and proved it was no barrier at all.

The 6,000-pounds thrust XLR-11 rocket engine that rammed the bullet-shaped vehicle into supersonic flight was small by comparison with today's giant spacecraft launchers, yet that achievement in 1947 was an important milestone. Some rate it as significant as the first wobbling flight of the Wright brothers' biplane at Kitty Hawk in 1903. It opened the door to an exciting new world of high-speed travel that would lead to the edge of space, to the moon, and to the planets beyond.

USAF Capt. Charles E. Yeager broke the sound barrier in 1947.

Douglas D-558-II research ship is drop-launched by B-29.

Almost forgotten today is the saga of these forerunners of space shuttles, the supersonic X planes that blasted the sound barrier and went on to conquer other barriers still more formidable. There was the searing heat barrier (sometimes called the *thermal thicket*) that could melt conventional aluminum jet planes by atmospheric friction alone. Scientists solved that problem with heat-resistant alloys of titanium, zirconium, molybdenum, and cobalt in building triple-sonic military craft like the B-70 and SR-71.

Once past the sonic and heat barriers, engineers were confronted with a new problem—the so-called controllability barrier—at the fringe of space. Aerodynamic controls (ailerons, rudder, and elevator) normally change an airplane's attitude by pushing against the rushing air, but they are useless where there is no air for them to push against. So devices called jet thrusters were developed for use when the pilots of research rocket ships fly above the atmosphere. Such devices are called reaction controls.

Lunar explorer Col. Edwin E. Aldrin heads USAF Aerospace Research Pilot School at Edwards Air Force Base.

Step by careful step, X plane pilots crossed the new frontiers of flight, rocketing toward the stars at thousands instead of hundreds of miles an hour, learning as they went. Death was their copilot on some flights when their fast craft whipped unexpectedly out of control, but this did not stop America's determined test pilots.

At Edwards Air Force Base, where Captain (now General) Yeager first flew faster than sound, an Aerospace Research Pilot School was established to pass along the knowledge gained to other test pilots who would follow. Progress was slow at first, but ahead lay a single goal—to push back the frontiers of flyable aircraft into space itself.

NASA pilot Neil A. Armstrong, first man on the moon, flew X-15 seven times, to 3,989 mph and 207,500 feet altitude. Other X-15 research pilots (l-r below) are Capt. William J. Knight, Lt. Col. Robert A. Rushworth, Capt. Joe Engle, Milton O. Thompson, William H. Dana, John B. McKay.

From the outset, pilots at both the USAF Flight Test Center and the National Aeronautics and Space Administration (NASA) Flight Research Center, which share the vast, dry, alkali lake bed at Edwards, recognized that their ultimate challenge was to build a national space transportation system, to rocket men and cargo into space and back on an efficiently economical and routine basis.

Once a Saturn V launches an Apollo spacecraft on a journey to the moon, nothing comes back except the Apollo command capsule. By 1971 nearly 5,000 pieces of space junk littered the skies, a matter of growing concern to future orbital traffic. Such waste put the cost of orbiting payloads to hundreds of thousands of dollars a pound. A space shuttle system would bring the cost down to less than one hundred dollars a pound, but economics alone did not dictate the need for a national space transportation system. There simply was no better way to convert our space exploits of the 1960's into scientific missions to be carried out for the benefit of all mankind.

Orbiting laboratories called space stations were already on the drawing boards, and hardware existed in 1971 for an Experimental Space Station (XSS)—Skylab. Clusters of space stations, called permanent space bases, also were being planned, where up to 100 men and women could live and work together on missions lasting for months and years.

At Edwards, prototype space shuttle aircraft were under development, to provide reusable space ferries for transporting passengers and cargo to the space stations and back. This program properly dates back to the XS-1 and its successor, the Bell X-2, which explored the realm of flight at three times the speed of sound and to altitudes above 126,000 feet.

While designers and test pilots wrestled with the perplexing problems of supersonic flight, in 1959 a strange new X plane took over the shuttle development program at Edwards—the North American X-15. Long and black and fitted with short, stubby wings, this research ship weighed 50,000 pounds and carried a rocket engine capable of delivering 70,000 pounds thrust, permitting it to accelerate in a near-vertical climb.

Target of the X-15 was the edge of space and flight speeds almost seven times the speed of sound, well into the realm of hypersonic flight, which begins at Mach 5 (five times the speed of sound). Three of these amazing craft flew a total of 199 missions in a $300,000,000 program, the proving ground for future manned space flight.

Fitted with rocket reaction controls, the X-15 was a hybrid aircraft-spacecraft that could fly equally well in or out of the atmosphere, much in the way a flying fish can maneuver in water or air. On its return from

Covered with white heat-resistant material, X-15 drops away from B-52 mother ship for the searing plunge through the "thermal thicket" at 4,520 mph, October 3, 1967. Major William J. Knight, USAF, was the pilot. Below, typical X-15 flight profile covers 261 miles in climb to the edge of space and back to land at Edwards Air Force Base Flight Test Center.

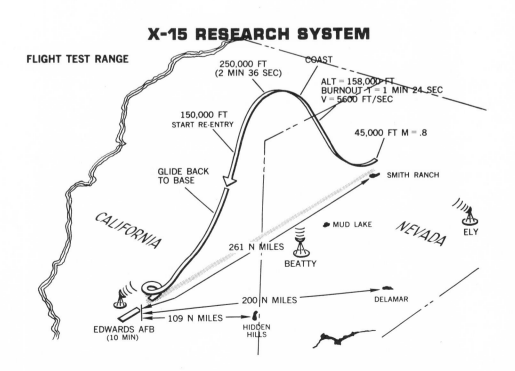

X-15 RESEARCH SYSTEM

FLIGHT TEST RANGE

COAST

250,000 FT
(2 MIN 36 SEC)

ALT = 158,000 FT
BURNOUT T = 1 MIN 24 SEC
V = 5600 FT/SEC

150,000 FT
START RE-ENTRY

45,000 FT M = .8

GLIDE BACK
TO BASE

SMITH RANCH

CALIFORNIA

MUD LAKE

NEVADA

ELY

261 N MILES

BEATTY

200 N MILES

DELAMAR

109 N MILES

HIDDEN
HILLS

EDWARDS AFB
(10 MIN)

X-15 wind tunnel model grows delta-shaped wings.

steep climbs of more than 67 miles, the X-15 glowed cherry red as it plunged earthward along a steep reentry corridor at 4,500 mph.

In addition to proving out materials and designs for space flight, the X-15s provided excellent space flight training for such future astronauts as the USAF's Joe H. Engle and NASA's Neil A. Armstrong, first man to set foot on the moon in 1969, just ten years after the X-15 program got under way.

Early in the X-15 program scientists also used it to carry a host of scientific experiments into space, collecting micrometeorites and photographing stars and the sun's corona. Looking to the future, wind-tunnel tests were conducted on a delta-shaped X-15 model with rugged triangular wings better suited to the requirements of hypersonic flight than conventional

Air Force X-20 Project Dyna-Soar with adapter section.

thin straight wings.

Following the X-15 program came a unique Air Force effort to develop a manned orbiting "space glider"—Project Dyna-Soar. Designated the X-20, Dyna-Soar was to have been boosted into orbit atop a multistage Titan III rocket as the United States' first maneuverable spacecraft. Orbiting over the poles, it would glide back into the upper atmosphere in a series of decelerating dips, gradually dissipating its energy to land without power on steel skids.

Dyna-Soar was finally scrapped as impractical, and in its place came a series of unusual wingless craft called lifting bodies (the searing heat would melt off conventional wings), built to explore the reentry problems of coming space shuttles.

History's first piloted wing-less aircraft was NASA's ply-wood M2-F1, with flat top, rounded bottom. It made successful powerless glides after being towed to 10,000 feet altitude, proved that lifting bodies could fly.

Veteran glider pilot Gus Briegleb (right) built the M2-F1 under NASA contract. Resembling a boat hull, this glider had zero wingspan, received lift from the unique shape of its body alone.

Nobody knew just what a wingless aircraft should look like. The first model, developed at NASA's Langley Research Center in Virginia, resembled a flying saucer. Next came the M-1 (first manned) version, shaped like a pyramid. NASA finally decided to make the M-2 flat on top and round on the bottom. Resembling a rowboat, it actually flew well as a glider.

The M-2 was conceived at NASA's Flight Research Center at Edwards, where most of the test pilots were soaring enthusiasts. It was built of plywood at a nearby glider base, El Mirage, by the Sailplane Corporation

Successor to plywood M2-F1 was this M2-F2, a 6,000-pound metal glider which maneuvered to a 200-mph landing after dropping from B-52 mother ship. An F-104 Starfighter flies "chase" at right.

M2-F2's unusual control system includes triple vertical fins and, at rear, combination elevator/ailerons called "elevons." Rocket thrusters were added for landing assist.

of America, and was towed into the air, first behind an automobile and then behind a DC-3.

NASA pilot Milt Thompson flew the M-2 on some 100 test flights, and in 1964 NASA contracted with Northrop Corporation to build a metal version, the M2-F2. Northrop also built a second lifting body, the HL-10 (tenth horizontal lander) which was flat-bottomed and rounded on top. Each was 22 feet long, weighed 2½ tons, and carried a more powerful XLR-11 rocket engine of 8,000 pounds thrust, plus four smaller rockets to assist the pilot on his landing approach.

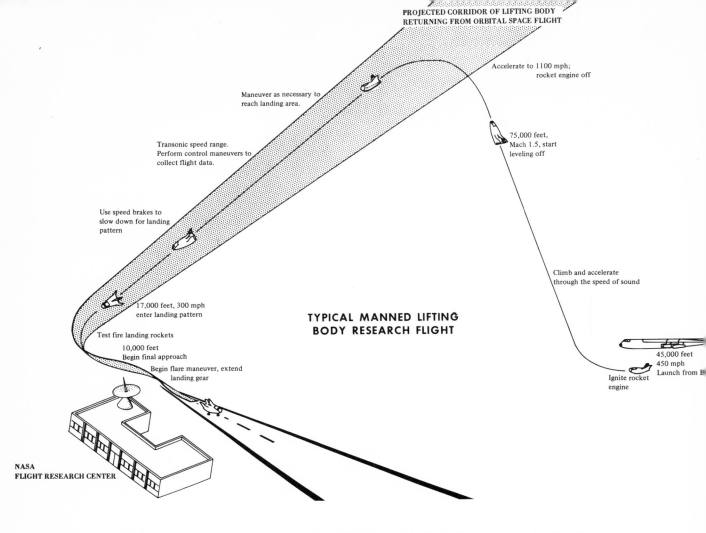

PROJECTED CORRIDOR OF LIFTING BODY
RETURNING FROM ORBITAL SPACE FLIGHT

Accelerate to 1100 mph;
rocket engine off

Maneuver as necessary to
reach landing area.

75,000 feet,
Mach 1.5, start
leveling off

Transonic speed range.
Perform control maneuvers to
collect flight data.

Use speed brakes to
slow down for landing
pattern

Climb and accelerate
through the speed of sound

**TYPICAL MANNED LIFTING
BODY RESEARCH FLIGHT**

17,000 feet, 300 mph
enter landing pattern

Test fire landing rockets

45,000 feet
450 mph
Launch from B

10,000 feet
Begin final approach

Ignite rocket
engine

Begin flare maneuver, extend
landing gear

NASA
FLIGHT RESEARCH CENTER

*Manned lifting body research flights are conducted at Edwards Air Force
Base to simulate flight characteristics of a space shuttle descending along
a high cross-range approach to landing after return from orbit.*

In flight it works this way: the lifting bodies are carried up to 45,000
feet beneath the wing of a B-52 and dropped at 450 mph. The pilot fires
his rocket engine and climbs to 75,000 feet, reaching 1,100 mph before
starting the glide back down a steep flight path, like the reentry corridor
of a space shuttle.

During this simulated reentry, the lifting body pilot makes a series of
turns, slowing down to subsonic flight speeds, using his dive brakes. He is
still more than three miles high when he enters the airport traffic pattern,
diving through an overhead turn to line up with the runway at 300 mph.

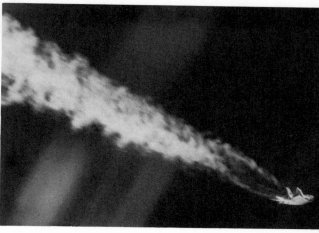

NASA test pilot John A. Manke rides Northrop HL-10 "flying flatiron" to 45,000 feet beneath B-52 mother ship, drops away and rockets to 80,000 feet at 1,000 mph, before diving back to land on dry lakebed at Edwards Air Force Base. F-104 "chase" plane follows him down.

He test fires his landing rockets to make sure they're working, then sails across the edge of the dry lake bed, still two miles up. Extending his landing gear, he swoops down to land like a diving hawk, nose held high.

This dangerous and difficult flight testing is carried out by a team of the world's finest pilots. Typical is Air Force Major Jerauld R. Gentry, who won the Harmon Trophy for making the first powered flight of the HL-10 on October 23, 1968. Another is NASA pilot William A. Dana, who reached Mach .8 on the first powered flight of the M2-F3 on November 25, 1970.

Air Force PRIME (Precision Recovery Including Maneuvering Entry) SV-5D reentry test vehicle streaks back into atmosphere at hypersonic speed after launch down Western Test Range atop Atlas SLV-3 rocket from Vandenberg Air Force Base.

The Air Force's lifting body research program, the X-24A, got under way in 1967 when a 7-foot model was launched from Vandenberg Air Force Base down the Pacific Test Range, atop an Atlas launch vehicle. Called the SV-5D, it was part of a program with the name PRIME (Precision Recovery Including Maneuvering Entry).

V-shaped, with a flat bottom, rounded top and vertical fins, made of aluminum, the SV-5D was coated with heat-resistant materials. It carried reaction controls for space flight, and split flaps under the tail for pitch and roll maneuvering in the atmosphere.

The first two PRIME models were lost at sea but returned valuable data

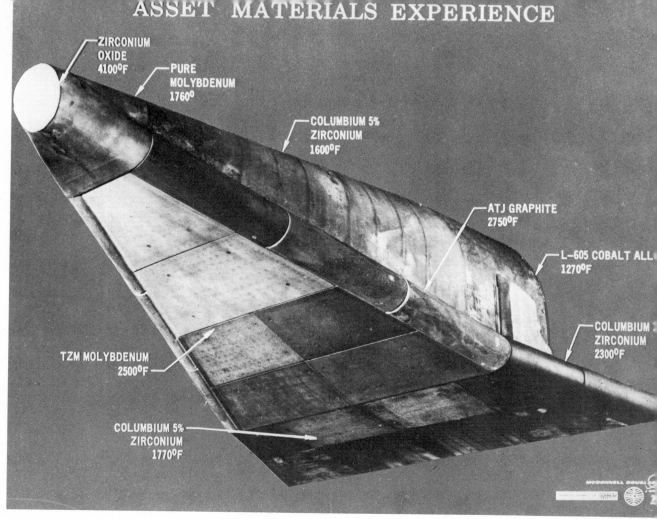

ZIRCONIUM
OXIDE
4100°F

PURE
MOLYBDENUM
1760°

COLUMBIUM 5%
ZIRCONIUM
1600°F

ATJ GRAPHITE
2750°F

L-605 COBALT ALL
1270°F

COLUMBIUM
ZIRCONIUM
2300°F

TZM MOLYBDENUM
2500°F

COLUMBIUM 5%
ZIRCONIUM
1770°F

McDonnell Douglas ASSET research lifting body was built of heat-resistant metals to determine best way to protect future space shuttles against incineration during reentry into earth's atmosphere at meteoric velocities.

by radio, while the third and fourth were recovered as they parachuted to earth near Kwajalein Island in Micronesia.

A different Air Force program, seeking further to define the shape of space shuttles, was Project START (Spacecraft Technology and Advanced Reentry Test), completed in 1965 after firing six test vehicles down the Eastern Test Range. These craft bore the acronym ASSET (Aerothermo-dynamic/elastic Structural Systems Environmental Test) and were used in a study of new heat shield materials for reusable space ferries.

Built by McDonnell Douglas, the delta-shaped ASSETS were made of radiative materials such as graphite, zirconium, columbium, and molybdenum, capable of withstanding temperatures up to 4000°F.

37

NASA test pilot John Manke, a modern knight in shining armor.

Following these early efforts, the Air Force moved to a manned version of the SV-5 shape, designated SV-5P and given the project name PILOT (PIloted LOwspeed Test). Later called the X-24A, this winged wonder became the latest of the USAF X plane series and, like NASA's lifting body craft, carried an XLR-11 rocket engine.

Although basically designed to simulate the flight of future space shuttles operating from orbit to land, the X-24A's prime mission was exploration of the lower speed regime from Mach 2 down to landing speeds.

NASA pilot John Manke observed the twenty-third anniversary of the first supersonic flight on October 14, 1970, by rocketing to Mach 1.1 in the X-24A, reaching an altitude of 66,000 feet before gliding back down the space-return corridor to an unpowered landing. The flight was routine, and therefore all the more remarkable, for it established the wingless wonders as the prototype of tomorrow's work horse space shuttles.

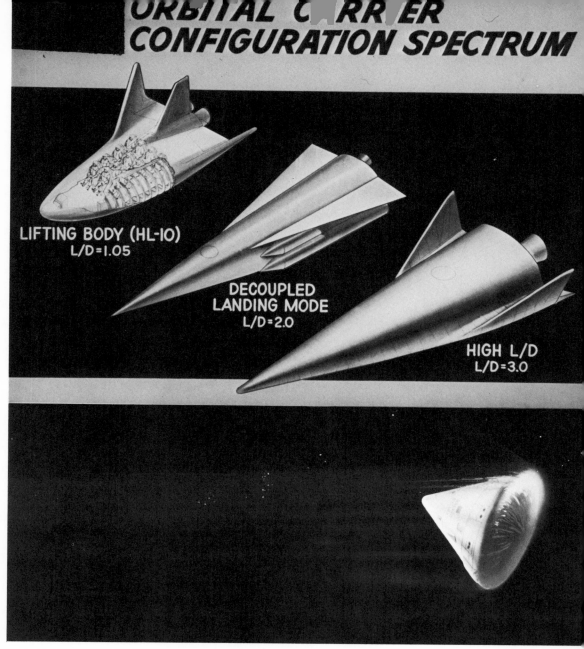

LIFTING BODY (HL-10)
L/D=1.05

DECOUPLED
LANDING MODE
L/D=2.0

HIGH L/D
L/D=3.0

Apollo Command Capsule.

In the near future, manned lifting bodies coated with heat-resistant materials will be flown through the entire shuttle mission from liftoff to earth orbit to landing, bringing back information that will serve as a blueprint for shuttle missions some years hence. Then the "flying flatirons" will be retired to museums, their job well done.

In the meantime, the last three capsules of the Apollo moon program in 1971 were assigned to serve as temporary shuttle craft in support of our first space station, Skylab. That story is told in the next chapter.

THE NEXT BIG STEP—SKYLAB

AMERICA'S IMAGINATIVE and challenging space exploration program seemed to have reached an incredible climax on the Sunday afternoon of July 20, 1969, when Apollo 11 Lunar Excursion Module *Eagle* settled to the surface of the moon in the desolate Sea of Tranquility, one year ahead of schedule.

Ever since President John F. Kennedy in 1961 committed the nation to a manned lunar landing in that decade, the full weight of the United States space effort had pressed toward that single goal. And great though the achievement was, it remained "one small step for man" in the broader picture of space exploration.

The successes of Apollo 11 and subsequent manned lunar missions were heralded as milestones of technology, but still to come were more meaningful achievements, capable of bringing richer returns for the benefit of all mankind.

A full year before the flight of Apollo 11, General James Ferguson, commander of the U.S. Air Force Systems Command, made clear that "the moon program was intended from the outset as a departure point . . . a mind-stretching venture . . . an experience-building enterprise. Perhaps," he said, "too many people have come to equate the lunar expedition with our total space program, or to think of it as an end rather than a beginning."

The bigger goal ahead was defined by NASA as " a full investigation of man's role in the effective exploitation of the environment of space, to meet man's needs on the Earth and in the long-term exploration of the Universe."

In other words, once man learned how to survive in the hostile void of outer space, using the moon as a proving ground, the stage was set to build permanent laboratories in space, where scientists could live, work, sleep, and relax while pursuing their ultimate search into the mysteries of nature beyond earth.

Man has dreamed of space travel for centuries, but only in this one has he mastered the various technologies of rocketry, electronics, and other disciplines needed to make it possible. Extended space travel is no longer a dream; plans are on the drawing boards, astronauts and scientists are in training, and actual hardware exists for long-term flights into space. Just as the technology of the 1960's was devoted to reaching the moon, so will this decade see the next giant step into space become reality—orbiting space stations.

Skylab Experimental Space Station.

S-IVB rocket stage becomes orbiting "mobile home."

Employing launch rockets and Apollo spacecraft left over from the moon missions, NASA's first-generation Experimental Space Station (XSS)—Skylab I—can be ready to go into earth orbit in 1973, using an empty Apollo third-stage launch rocket casing for its outer shell.

Called the S-IVB, this casing, the size of a three-bedroom house, will provide 10,000 cubic feet of living space for three astronauts who will spend up to 56 days per mission inside it.

Toward the end of the decade, when designs for space living have been worked out in Skylab flights, still larger space stations may stay in orbit for as long as ten years, resupplied periodically by sophisticated space shuttles called Advanced Logistic System spacecraft.

Extended manned space flights were proven feasible in 1965 when Astronauts Frank Borman and James Lovell flew the Gemini 7 capsule through a record 220 orbits in 330.6 hours—nearly two weeks in space. Fears of micrometeorite strikes, cosmic and solar radiation, and other "space sickness syndromes" receded, yet only by doubling and quadrupling the lengths of orbital stay-time could we learn whether man can adapt fully to living in space, particularly in a zero-gravity (weightless) state.

In California, the McDonnell Douglas Corporation in the late 1960's tackled the problem of how to turn empty S-IVB rocket stages into orbital workshops once they were in orbit, by purging them of hydrogen gas fumes. Called the Apollo Applications Program (AAP), the concept later became the Skylab program. Dr. George Mueller, NASA's associated administrator for manned space flight, called Skylab "an effort even more important and far-reaching in its applications than the Apollo effort upon which it is based."

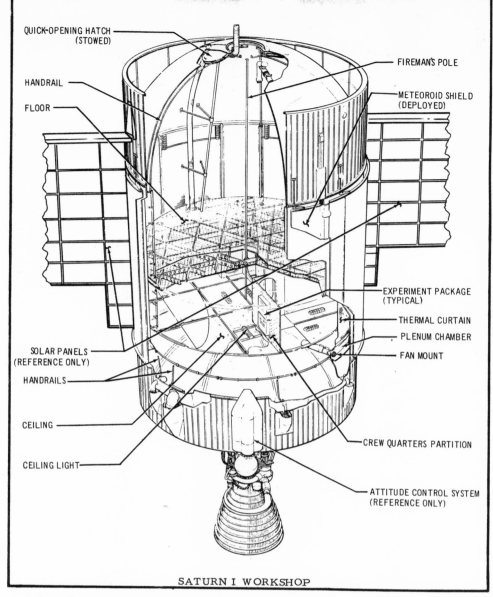

QUICK-OPENING HATCH
(STOWED)

HANDRAIL

FLOOR

FIREMAN'S POLE

METEOROID SHIELD
(DEPLOYED)

EXPERIMENT PACKAGE
(TYPICAL)

THERMAL CURTAIN

PLENUM CHAMBER

FAN MOUNT

SOLAR PANELS
(REFERENCE ONLY)

HANDRAILS

CEILING

CEILING LIGHT

CREW QUARTERS PARTITION

ATTITUDE CONTROL SYSTEM
(REFERENCE ONLY)

SATURN I WORKSHOP

The idea of reusing spent rocket casings to build up a modular space station in orbit is not new—Dr. Krafft Ehricke in 1959 proposed using a spent Atlas casing for a Skylab. The concept was revived at Douglas and submitted to Dr. Wernher von Braun, director of NASA's Marshall Space Flight Center. Engineers initially proposed that astronauts live inside an empty and unpressurized S-IVB rocket casing in extra-vehicular activity (EVA) pressure suits, but it seemed a better idea to pressurize the casing at 5 pounds per square inch, to create a shirt-sleeve nitrogen-oxygen environment, similar to the atmosphere you'd find at a high mountain resort.

Heart of the Skylab Experimental Space Station is the S-IVB casing itself, called the Saturn Workshop. It is fitted with grilled aluminum flooring and partitions to provide living quarters and work space. Shaped like a giant beer can, the casing is 58.4 feet tall and 21.7 feet in diameter.

Air Force Manned Orbiting Laboratory (MOL) was to have launched from Vandenberg Air Force Base with two strapon boosters (left), placing pair of USAF astronauts into polar orbit aboard Gemini B spacecraft attached to nose (above). After 30-day stay in space they were to return aboard the Gemini capsule. MOL project was ultimately abandoned.

While the NASA mission in space exploration is a peaceful one, the Air Force showed interest in Skylab and tentatively pursued a parallel research program of its own, called Manned Orbiting Laboratory (MOL). The MOL military space station, actually meant only to determine man's role in space in terms of national defense, was to have consisted of a laboratory and experiment module to which a Gemini B two-man spacecraft could dock. Two USAF astronauts would spend 30 days inside a small 10-by-42-foot cylinder, placed into orbit from Vandenberg Air Force Base in California atop a Titan missile launcher. After spending more than two-thirds of a billion dollars on MOL, the USAF scrapped the project, largely because Skylab could do the research job just as well.

Skylab space station will be manned by three scientists for up to 56 days in orbit. From left: Apollo command capsule which serves as space ferry; Multiple Docking Adapter to which additional experiment modules can attach; Air Lock Module; Saturn I Workshop. Wing-like panels convert sunlight into electricity.

Skylab emerged as a modular space station to be assembled in orbit instead of launched as a single unit. Attached to the central Workshop module is a specially designed Air Lock Module, about 16½ feet long. The Air Lock will be the Skylab's "nerve center," to accommodate two of the three astronauts in pressure suits, enabling them to exit into space for extra-vehicular activity (EVA) without depressurizing the Workshop.

On the opposite end of the Air Lock will be another cylinder, to which arriving and departing Apollo capsules will attach in docking maneuvers. Called the Multiple Docking Adapter, this unit will contain about 1,500 cubic feet of storage area and room for certain crew operations. A pair of windows will allow the crew to look outside the Docking Adapter, to

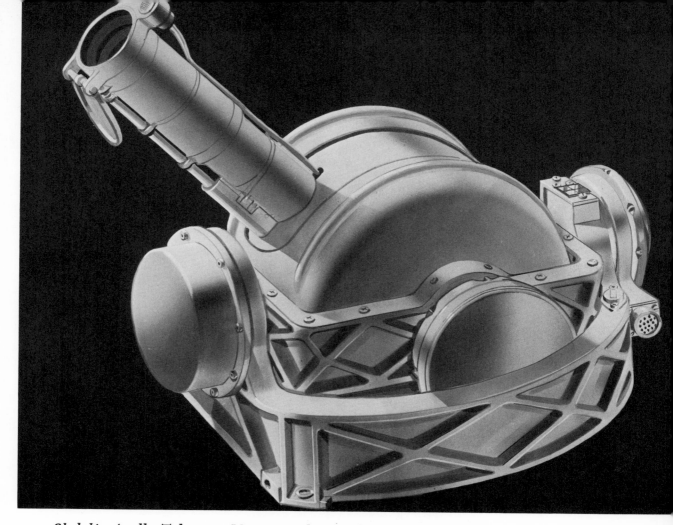

Skylab's Apollo Telescope Mount can be aimed precisely by Bendix automatic star-tracker which "locks onto" such navigation stars as Canopus or Achernar. Telescopes will be stabilized by three 400-pound gyroscopes spinning at 8,000 rpm.

observe the Skylab's most important experimental device, the Apollo Telescope Mount.

The Telescope Mount will launch from earth inside the Workshop, and once in orbit will be swung outside on gimbals, so that both optical and radio telescopes may be precisely aimed at the sun or specific parts of the cosmos to be studied in orbit.

The telescopic unit—the United States' first manned orbital observatory—will be built around a one-half-ton tube, 48 inches in diameter and 10 feet long. The pointing mechanism and motor-driven cameras attached to the telescopes will be powered by wing-like panels containing hundreds of solar cells (solar arrays) to convert sunlight into electricity.

Star Field Tracker developed by The Martin Company will orient space station in flight by reading star patterns and selecting proper pointing axis in space.

Skylab astronauts will be able to train the NASA-developed telescopes on the sun and stars and for the first time view these celestial objects unobscured by the earth's blanket of air. In the Telescope Mount will be eight sensing instruments, which will be used to conduct five special experiments on the initial mission, measuring the sun's radiation in ultra-violet and X-ray bands which do not reach the earth's surface. Pictures also will be taken of the sun's visible corona.

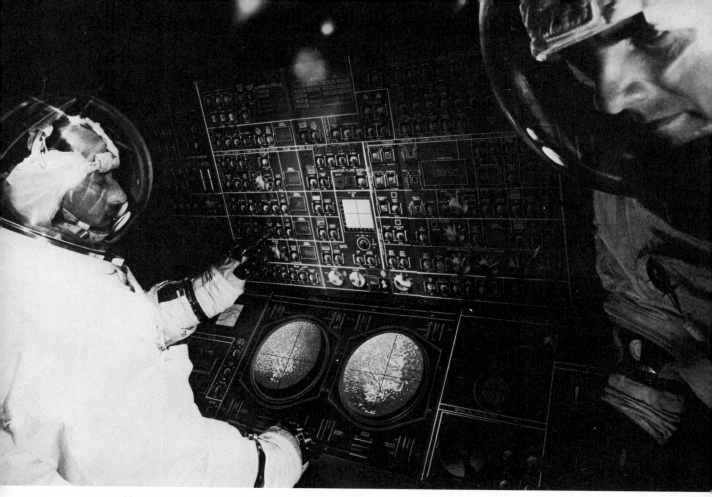

Apollo Telescope Mount's intricate primary control panel and display board, located inside Skylab's Multiple Docking Adapter, will be manned by two astronauts.

To operate the telescopes, two astronauts inside the Docking Adapter will study the heavens on a pair of TV display screens, precisely point the telescopes, snap pictures, then don pressure suits to go outside and change the film in the cameras. The telescopes are to be stabilized by three heavy gyroscopes, each weighing 400 pounds and spinning at 8,000 rpm. Just as observatories on earth lock their telescopes on specific stars as the earth turns, so orbiting telescopes must be locked onto what they are viewing by motor-driven devices. Power for this function will come from the solar arrays.

A second pair of solar array "wings" attached to Skylab, each 30-by-30 feet in area, will produce 12 kilowatts of power to run other systems inside the Workshop.

Crew System Evaluation Laboratory is engineering mock-up for Skylab-A, in which interior arrangement of living quarters and scientific experiment area is carefully planned prior to launch into orbit.

About 50 additional experiments have been suggested for study inside the Skylab. Some are biomedical, to study how well man can adapt to long stays in space, while others are earth-oriented, such as multi-spectral photography, a technique originally developed for use aboard Earth Resources Technology Satellites (ERTS) to inventory dwindling natural resources aboard "spaceship earth."

Inside Crew System Evaluation Laboratory scientists and engineers col-laborate in designing sleeping restrainers, exercycles, and storage areas, mounted on grilled aluminum flooring.

One curious experiment will be a study of cosmic radiations which come into the solar system from distant star fields of the Milky Way. These rays seldom reach the surface of the earth but are believed to be the cause of curious "firefly" light flashes reported seen by astronauts. It is believed the bright flashes occur when high-energy cosmic neutrons and helium atoms dart through the retinas of human eyes.

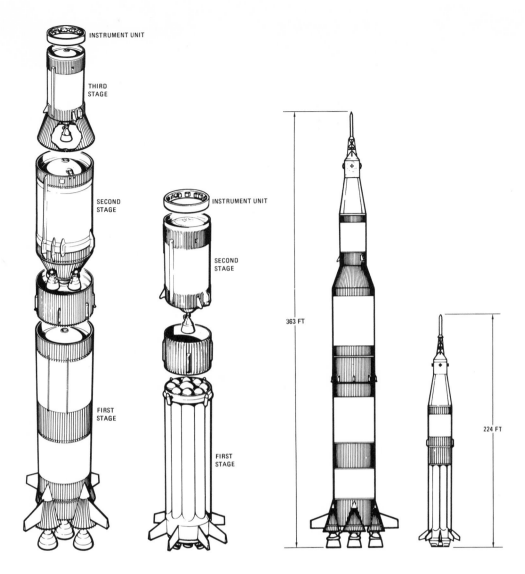

INSTRUMENT UNIT

THIRD STAGE

SECOND STAGE

FIRST STAGE

INSTRUMENT UNIT

SECOND STAGE

FIRST STAGE

363 FT

224 FT

Saturn V (left) and Saturn IB

Finally, a number of technological experiments are planned to learn how body movement by crew members may disturb the accuracy of telescope aiming; whether molten metal will form into perfect ball bearings in a zero-gravity state; and whether small gyroscopes attached to the backs of astronauts will help them to move about while weightless.

Most of these experiments will be launched aboard the Skylab when the mission begins from Complex 39 at Cape Kennedy. The first two stages of a Saturn V rocket will place the Skylab in a 235-mile-high orbit. Some 48 hours later the three-man Skylab crew will launch from nearby Complex 34 in an Apollo capsule, atop a Saturn IB.

After rendezvous in orbit with Skylab, the crew will enter the Saturn Workshop through the Air Lock, turn on the electrical power system,

He lost his mind in space! Bonny, male pigtail Macaque monkey, died from heart failure after 8 days of a 30-day programmed space flight. Brain-wave recordings led researchers to conclude Bonny's brain became detached in prolonged weightless state. Disrupted biological body rhythms in zero gravity may pose serious problems for astronauts on extended space missions, say UCLA researchers.

swing the big Telescope Mount outside, pressurize the Workshop, and settle down for a one-month stay.

When the crew's 28-day stay in space is finished, they will shut down the space station's power systems, reenter the Apollo module, and return to earth. The next four weeks will be spent evaluating the mission, prior to sending up the next crew. The second and third Skylab teams may stay in orbit as long as 56 days each.

Programmed as an interim effort between the Apollo lunar missions and future space station missions of the late 1970's, Skylab is under the control of the NASA Marshall Space Flight Center in Alabama. What is learned from Skylab will determine the final shape of the first permanent 12-man space station, described in the following chapter.

LIFE ABOARD A SPACE STATION

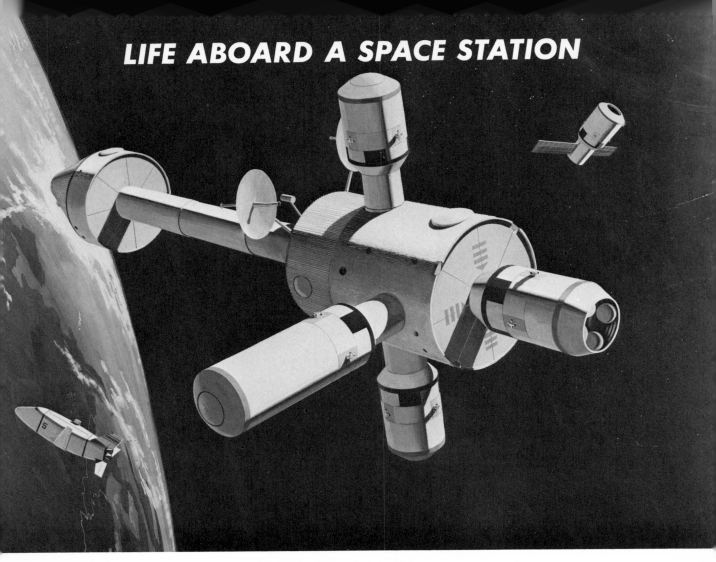

12-man permanent space station of late 1970's.

BY THE END of this decade, with the experience of Skylab space station flights behind them, space scientists will be ready to move into the United States' first permanent orbiting laboratory, a 12-man satellite with an expected lifetime of at least ten years.

The forerunner of future 100-man space bases, it will be assembled in orbit from modular sections, like a giant Tinker Toy, the whole thing rotating slowly to create an artificial gravity. Sophisticated space shuttles, called Advanced Logistic System (ALS) craft, will visit the station periodically, bringing up fresh supplies and rotating the mission scientists every 90 to 180 days.

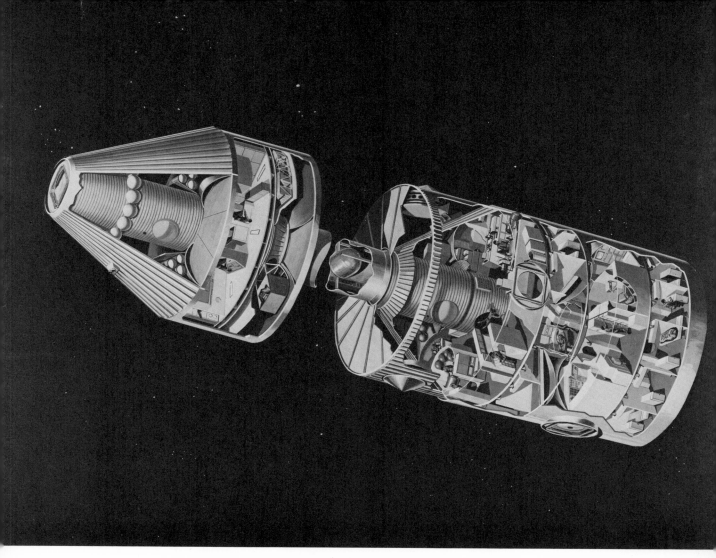

Cutaway view of 12-man permanent space station.

As yet, scientists are unsure how well man can adapt to life in a zero-gravity environment for extended periods; this can only be determined through actual experience. To settle the matter, the McDonnell Douglas Astronautics Company, builder of the Skylab XSS experimental space station, has designed a unique artificial-gravity concept.

In this design, an artificial-gravity module will be extended from the end of a telescopic tunnel which will run the full 111-foot length of the space station, to act as a counterbalance as the whole station is rotated by firing propulsion rockets.

Spinning at four revolutions per minute, the passengers will experience

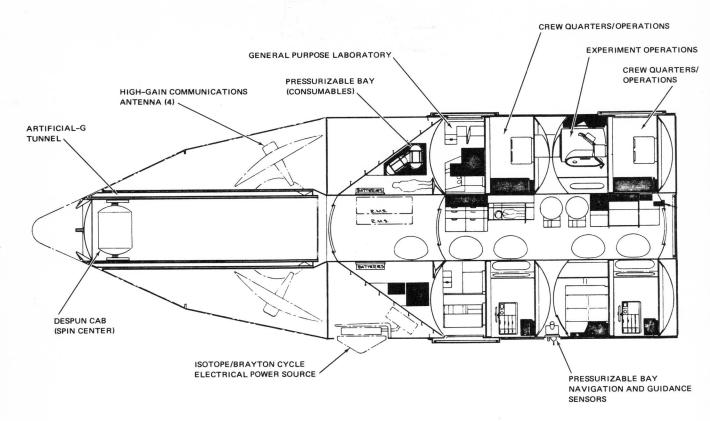

CREW QUARTERS/OPERATIONS

EXPERIMENT OPERATIONS

CREW QUARTERS/
OPERATIONS

GENERAL PURPOSE LABORATORY

PRESSURIZABLE BAY
(CONSUMABLES)

HIGH–GAIN COMMUNICATIONS
ANTENNA (4)

ARTIFICIAL-G
TUNNEL

DESPUN CAB
(SPIN CENTER)

ISOTOPE/BRAYTON CYCLE
ELECTRICAL POWER SOURCE

PRESSURIZABLE BAY
NAVIGATION AND GUIDANCE
SENSORS

*Plan view of 12-man space station shows interior of 50-foot core module
(right) and artificial gravity module (left) which extends overall length
of station to 111 feet when in use.*

much the same sensation as in a walk on the moon, the gravity pull of
which is one-sixth that of earth. A faster rotation would increase the
strength of the simulated gravity. The artificial-gravity experiment will
not be undertaken until scientists aboard the space station have had a
90-day period to become accustomed to weightlessness. This will provide
comparative data on which to base a decision whether or not to design
artificial-gravity systems for future 100-man space bases.

The initial 12-man space station will be launched into a high orbit of
perhaps 55 degrees, at an altitude of 246 miles in order to provide
maximum coverage for earth-oriented experiments. This way, for example,
special cameras will be able to cover most of the earth's land masses for
natural resource surveys and antipollution studies.

Some 48 hours after the station is placed in orbit an Advanced Logistic System shuttle will be launched to carry the initial 12-man station crew to rendezvous and docking. The shuttle will move around the station for a close inspection of its exterior, then two men will don pressure suits and enter the station to set up housekeeping.

This task will be similar to preparing a Skylab space station for human occupancy, much like reopening a house after an extended absence. Air conditioning must be turned on to provide a normal atmosphere, auxiliary power units started to provide power for lights and communications, and the air lock readied for the others to come inside.

Setting up housekeeping in 12-man space station.

A hotel in space! Cutaway view of central core of 12-man space station showing crew quarters, command and control areas in upper part, laboratory-experiment area, and physical conditioning area. Round openings at top and bottom are multiple docking ports to accept logistics shuttle craft. A free-flying experiment module can be seen at lower left.

Primary control center on space station's second deck.

A thorough check of every part of the station will be made by the men to insure that all is in good working order. The station, 54 feet from end to end, will be 33 feet in diameter. The interior volume of 32,800 cubic feet will be divided by partitions into four deck levels, a cellar, and an attic.

In the basement will be heavy equipment such as fans and blowers, placed there to isolate their noise from the sleeping and working quarters. The basement will also contain bulk storage space for food, water, and other supplies.

On the first deck are to be the galley, wardroom, a medical laboratory and dispensary, and a first aid station. There will be six staterooms on each of the next two decks, equipped with work areas, television sets, showers and hygiene facilities, and even radio-telephones to call home.

A primary control center, manned by two men, will occupy part of

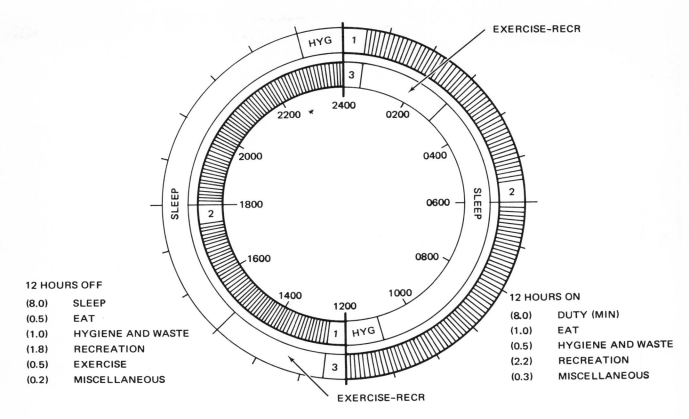

EXERCISE-RECR

HYG 1

3

2400
2200 2400 0200
2000 0400
SLEEP 1800 0600 SLEEP 2
2 1800 0600
1600 0800
1400 1000
1200

HYG 1

3

EXERCISE-RECR

12 HOURS OFF

(8.0)	SLEEP
(0.5)	EAT
(1.0)	HYGIENE AND WASTE
(1.8)	RECREATION
(0.5)	EXERCISE
(0.2)	MISCELLANEOUS

12 HOURS ON

(8.0)	DUTY (MIN)
(1.0)	EAT
(0.5)	HYGIENE AND WASTE
(2.2)	RECREATION
(0.3)	MISCELLANEOUS

Two-shift duty cycle. Flight crews in space will work on two daily 12-hour tours with six men assigned to each tour. Work week covers 56 hours, eight hours a day. Men will divide their time into three daily eight-hour periods of rest, recreation, and work.

the second deck, with an experimental secondary control center on the floor above. Deck four will contain the space experiment area, the air lock, and photographic, physics, and optics facilities. In the attic will be other noisy pieces of equipment, such as auxiliary power units and fuel for attitude control thrusters.

With possible variations, this design concept permits a feeling of roominess while still affording privacy for both rest and recreation periods. The crew members will divide their time into three daily eight-hour periods for rest, recreation, and work, the latter involving both experimental program monitoring and station-keeping tasks.

A wide variety of space experiments has already been suggested by universities, government agencies, and others who will be using the space station for research projects. One plan calls for ten separate experiments to be integrated within the station, eight attached to it as modules, and another ten free-flying close to the station, under its control.

World's largest artificial-gravity simulator is this rotational facility at North American Rockwell, with 40-foot crew module built from a surplus USAF KC-97 fuselage, mounted on 160-foot diameter beam. Four men ride the simulator at 4 rpm. No discomfort was found in week-long rides.

Zero gravity will take some getting used to, in such everyday activities as hand washing, showering, and shaving. In a space station shower bath, water would remain suspended without something like a suction fan to suck it down into a floor drain.

At least there will be no lumpy bed problems, for the men will be floating in their sleep under elasticized nets covering blankets, to prevent them from drifting off into slumberland and banging their heads on the ceiling!

Following completion of the first 90-day weightless period, the artificial-gravity module will be extended and the space station spun up for another 90-day period. The artificial-gravity experiments will have three basic objectives:

• Mimimizing or eliminating illusions and disorientation of any crew members who show evidence of the phenomenon called *space sickness syndrome.*

• Prevention of body changes in musculo-skeletal, cardiovascular, and fluid balance systems within the crew.

• Establishment of the optimum spin rate of the artificial-gravity module for crew operations.

The artificial-gravity experiments will be conducted five times in the first 15 months of flight—once every three months, with a fresh crew each time—to obtain comparative biomedical data on a total of 60 people.

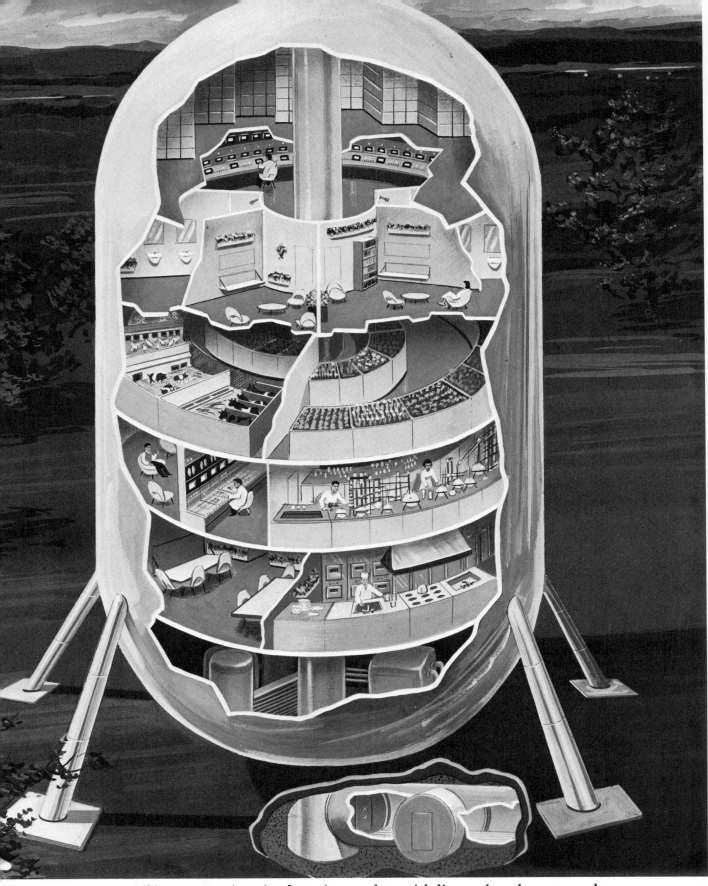

This space station simulator is complete with livestock and green garden produce, kitchen, laboratory, control center, and recreation rooms.

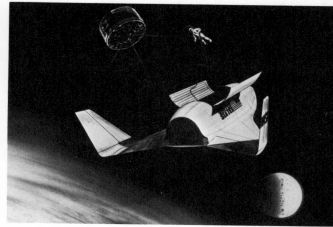
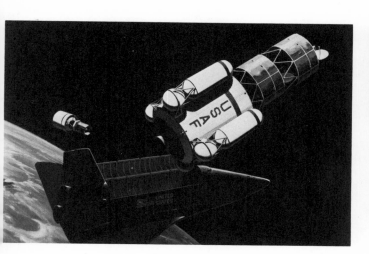

Space shuttles can be used to place communications satellites in orbit, inspect malfunctioning satellites, deliver multiple military satellites into high-altitude orbits, or launch interplanetary probes.

During the space station's ten-year lifetime, new experimental modules will be brought up from earth by ALS shuttle craft and docked by remotely-guided self-propulsion, while other Free-Flying Modules (FFM's) will be dispatched to function as robot stellar observatories, independently probing secrets of the universe and storing the data for later retrieval. Periodically, the FFM's will be recalled for refueling, routine maintenance and resupply, and data collection.

When an experiment module has served its purpose it will be returned to earth in the cargo bay of a shuttle craft, which on the same flight brings up a replacement module, thus permitting an economical and continuous program of scientific space research over the station's ten-year lifetime.

INFLATABLE MID-TORSO RESTRAINT

LEG RAIL RESTRAINT

SUCTION SHOES

LINEAR INDUCTION MOBILE HANDHOLD

PORTABLE HANDRAIL

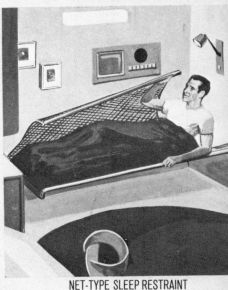
NET-TYPE SLEEP RESTRAINT

MOBILITY AND RESTRAINT DEVICE CONCEPTS
FOR FUTURE MANNED SPACE SYSTEMS

Like the captain of a ship, the space station commander will have full authority over all operations. Under the commander will be a physician, an operations director, and an experiment director, each with his own area of responsibility. Other experiment scientists, a station controller, and a cook/steward/engineer will complete the duty assignment roster.

Living in space will be an exciting adventure and an arduous existence as well. Flight crews will work on two daily 12-hour tours with six men assigned to each tour. The work week will cover 56 hours, eight hours a day, with flexible shift changes allowed as necessary.

"PERSONAL LIVING QUARTERS FOR FUTURE
LONG DURATION SPACE MISSIONS"

There will be plenty to do on board a space station. Whirling around
the earth once every 90 minutes, one can look down upon virtually every
habitable part of the globe, under a black canopy of sky filled with
myriad star clusters.

On earth, a microfilm library will store all necessary data for operation
of the space station, constantly updated by crew input. Besides the space
station itself, a giant network of support facilities will be part of the
program, including the Launch Control Center, Mission Management,
Data Relay Satellite System, and Tracking Network.

Three communications satellites, spaced equally apart around the earth, will provide a constant voice link, and on earth the tracking stations will keep a close watch on the space station's orbit until the onboard navigation system can take over.

From time to time shuttle craft will return to earth with exposed films, specimens, tissue samples, log books, photo-micrographs, and computer readouts, including data from the free-flying modules. This will take time—videograph pictures from the remote telescopes will require 90 minutes per frame for transmission to the space station.

Among the interesting possibilities now under study is a new type of docking device called the *androgynous* system (neither male nor female), which would enable any spacecraft to dock with any other spacecraft. This would permit an international cooperative sharing of future space stations by teams of scientists from both the United States and Russia, so that U.S. shuttles could dock at Russian space stations, and vice versa. Such a system would be invaluable during an emergency in space.

Sharing of space facilities could well be the forerunner of an international space patrol, functioning as a global monitoring agency, with the responsibility for bringing all wars to a halt and ending the misuse of the earth's dwindling supply of natural resources.

In the field of space technology, new breakthroughs may be achieved aboard space stations in the manufacture of products impossible to make on earth—for example, materials with the strength of steel and weight of balsa wood may be formed by pumping gas through molten steel in a zero-gravity state to create a hard, spongelike substance useful in spacecraft construction.

Unquestionably, important medical benefits will come from the application of space station science. It has been suggested that cardiac cases could be helped to a speedier recovery in an orbital hospital, where the patient's heart would be freed from the task of pumping blood through the circulatory system against gravity.

What other scientific and technological benefits mankind may expect from space station research can only be guessed at, but, properly directed, this new science will be more than worth the billions of dollars it will cost. Just as our space technology of the 1960's was dedicated to putting a man on the moon, so, in the 1970's, a more important goal exists—dedicating man's permanent role in space to achieving peace on earth.

Man is not likely to be soon replaced in space missions by robots. Despite the rapid advances in computer technology, sophisticated electronics devices capable of intelligent decision-making do not appear likely

Lockheed modular space base concept for the 1980's.

before the year 2,000, says NASA. Russian scientists, despite their successes with automated moon landers, agree that manned space research has become one of the most essential factors in the modern technological revolution.

Leonid I. Sedov, a founder of the Soviet space program, writes that international space cooperation is of paramount importance to all mankind. "In the face of the grandeur of the cosmos," says Sedov, "people begin to become aware of all the madness of bloody conflicts, brought about by aggressive interests. Therefore, space research not only helps deepen understanding of nature, and not only moves technology forward, but promotes wide international cooperation, mutual understanding, and the cause of peace in the whole world."

Man's widening awareness of the universe around him is not limited to nearby space; the vast solar system itself stands as our next challenge. In the next chapter the possibility of visiting other planets is assessed.

TO THE DISTANT PLANETS

100-man space base visits Mars, 1980's.

WILL ORBITING space bases and moon missions be the limit of man's venture into space, or will they serve as proving grounds from which man will go "one step beyond" to the distant planets?

The latter is most likely, according to a Space Task Group report to the President of the United States in September, 1969, in which guidelines were laid down for a post-Apollo Space Program.

Manned exploration of the planets, the report concluded, is the most challenging and most comprehensive of the many long-range goals available. In this grand venture, it said, "we have a unique opportunity to pursue a number of major questions man has asked about his relation to the universe. What is the history of the formation and evolution of the solar system? Are there clues to the origin of life? Does life exist elsewhere in the solar system?"

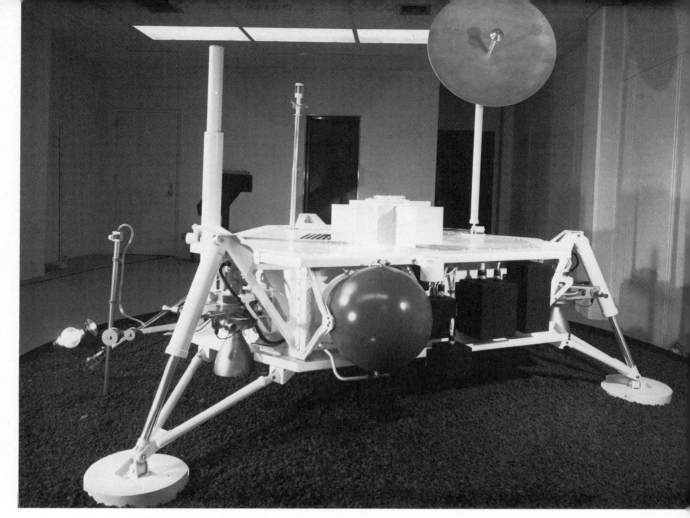

Viking interplanetary probe to land on Mars in 1975.

Before man ventures into deep space beyond the moon, unmanned planetary exploration missions will continue throughout this decade, both for return of new scientific knowledge and, in the case of Mars and Venus, as precursors to later manned missions.

Already we have learned much about Mars, the planet most likely to support life, from pictures returned in 1968 by Mariner spacecraft flybys. Martian craters are unlike those found on the moon, and the planet's rugged, chaotic terrain leads scientists to believe Mars is now much like Earth was in its early period.

Two new Mariners were programmed to orbit Mars in late 1971 for still closer looks, while in 1975 a pair of Viking planetary explorers will be launched, to arrive at Mars one year later. Each Viking will be a double spacecraft, consisting of a Mariner 1971-class orbiter, and a

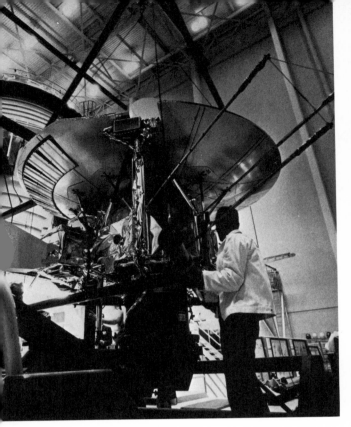

Jupiter spacecraft (left) will fly past the biggest planet in solar system following launch in 1972-73, returning data from 9-foot dish antenna by "radioisotope thermoelectric generator" power. Future manned interplanetary space bases may use nuclear power from reactor such as this SNAP 8DR at right.

Surveyor-type soft lander, similar to the Surveyors which landed on the moon.

Beyond Mars, NASA plans to launch two unmanned Pioneer spacecraft for a close look at Jupiter, largest planet of the solar system, nearly 11 times the diameter of Earth. One launch is scheduled for 1972, the other for 1974. These probes will travel half a billion miles in from 600 to 900 days, passing through the mysterious asteroid belt which may be a hazard to future manned interplanetary travel.

Flying so far away from the sun, conventional solar cell panels would be useless; in their place the Pioneers will carry four nuclear power sources called radioisotope thermoelectric generators. After a week orbiting the giant planet, they will soar off, deep into the region of the Milky Way.

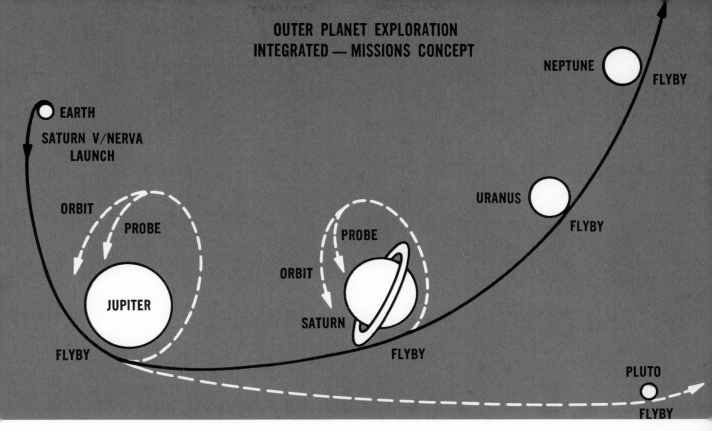

OUTER PLANET EXPLORATION
INTEGRATED — MISSIONS CONCEPT

"Grand Tour" of giant outer planets will utilize their huge gravity pull to swing a scientific satellite from one past the next on flyby visits to Jupiter, Saturn, Uranus, Neptune, and Pluto in the late 1970's.

In 1973 another planetary probe will be launched on a trip past the two planets closest to the sun, Venus and Mercury, and late in the decade will come the most challenging unmanned voyage of all—the so-called Grand Tour of the four outer planets.

This project, originated at the Jet Propulsion Laboratory in California, will take advantage of an unusual alignment of Jupiter, Saturn, Uranus, Neptune, and Pluto in the 1976-80 period. With the exception of Pluto, of which little is known, the outer planets differ radically in almost every respect from Mercury, Venus, Earth, and Mars, being of gigantic size (4 to 11 times the size of Earth), low in density ($\frac{1}{8}$ to $\frac{1}{4}$ that of Earth), and shrouded in dense atmospheres of hydrogen, helium, methane, and ammonia gases.

The success of the Grand Tour missions—four are planned—depends

Astronomers hope to get a close look at mysterious rings surrounding Saturn during Grand Tour of the outer planets.

on how well the missions use the gravity pull of one planet to accelerate and swing off, with enough energy to reach the next, like "cracking the whip."

These spacecraft flights will seek to explain a number of mysteries that have confounded astronomers for centuries, such as the nature of Jupiter's red spot, and Saturn's rings. More important to future manned interplanetary flights will be the en-route study of such flight hazards as asteroids and comets, the violence of solar winds, and the incredible intensity of Jupiter's radiation belts, a million times stronger than Earth's.

These unmanned flights will of course be supplemented by space station stellar observations with both optical and radio telescopes, able to pierce for the first time the great cosmic dust clouds that obscure 90 percent of the universe from viewers on earth.

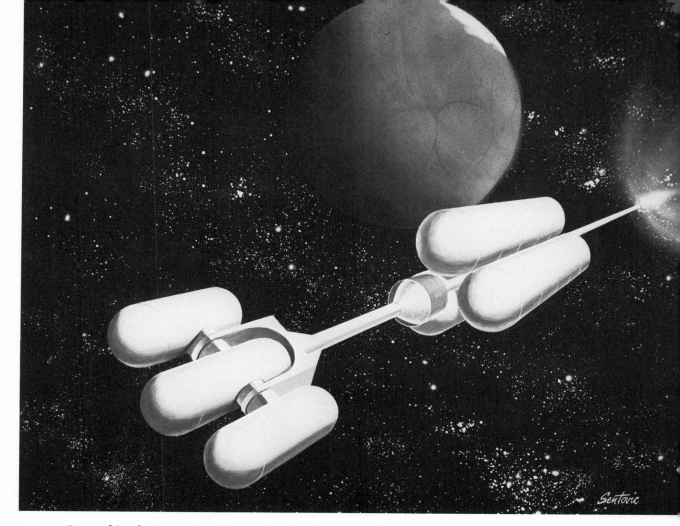

Spaceship designer Krafft A. Ehricke designed this nuclear-powered inter-planetary reconnaissance vehicle in 1961, for a 350-day manned visit to Mars and return.

Measurements also will be made from space stations of the phenomenon called zodiacal light, a cone of brightness that appears in the earth's twilight zone during the equinoxes. The glow is thought to be reflected sunlight from clouds of cosmic dust.

NASA now has plans that include a manned Mars mission in 1981, with a decision date by 1974, should the nation accept this mission as a commitment. Before that date we must depend on Skylab flights to study the biomedical aspects, both physiological and psychological, of flights lasting 500-600 days.

While scientists and engineers concern themselves with sophisticated nuclear and electrostatic propulsion systems for interplanetary spacecraft, others ask questions about the possibility of finding life elsewhere in the universe, and about the origin of the universe itself.

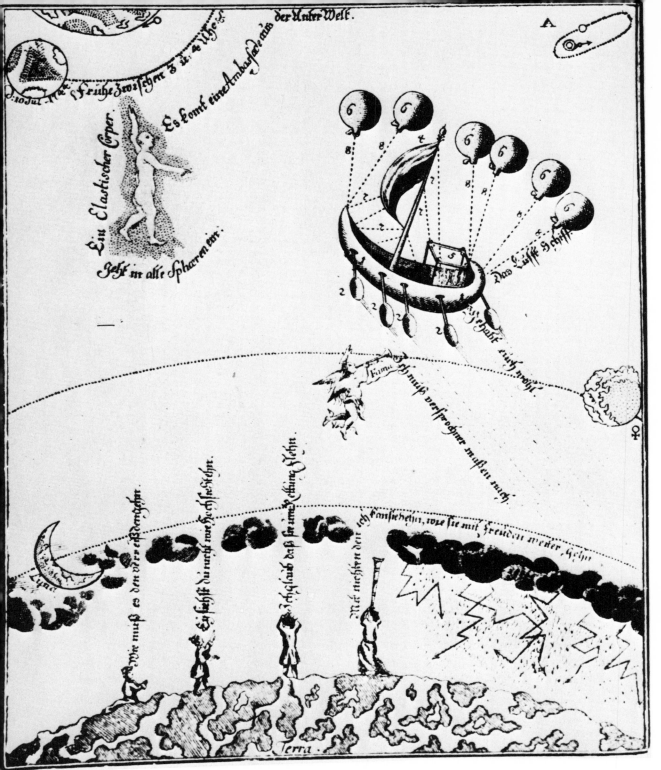

More than two centuries ago this imaginative scheme for interplanetary travel was proposed in a 1744 sketch, using 25-foot diameter copper spheres containing vacuums for lifting force. Vacuum-balloon scheme originated with Francisco Lana (1631-1687), a Jesuit priest.

Sir Bernard Lovell, noted British astronomer, believes the universe abounds in planets able to support organic evolution.

Sir Bernard Lovell, director of the Jodrell Bank radio telescope at Manchester, England, points out that while only a few percent of all the stars in our Milky Way galaxy might have planets able to sustain some form of organic evolution, "in the observable universe there are probably some trillion stars possessing planets in a suitable condition for the support of organic evolution."

Meteorite studies, Sir Bernard goes on to say, have revealed the presence of hydrocarbons and complex organic molecules. More recently, Dr. Cyril A. Ponnamperuma of NASA's Ames Research Center, announced the first positive identification of amino acids of extraterrestrial origin. The amino

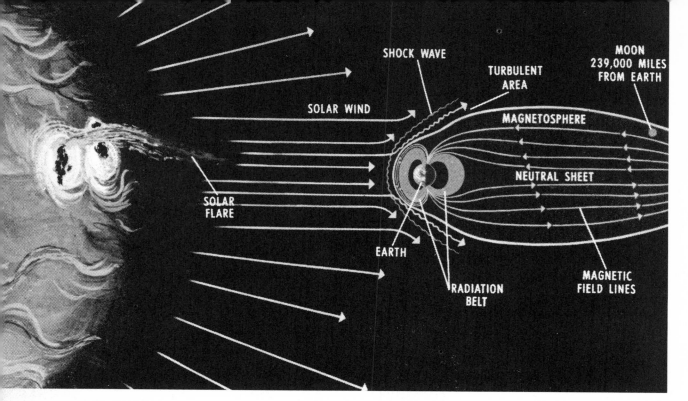

Future interplanetary space travelers will confront mysterious solar winds of plasma that may extend to the distant reaches of the solar system. Solar wind blows earth's magnetosphere away from sun, like the tail of a comet. Little is known of its true nature.

acids, principal constituents of living cells, were found in abundance in a meteorite which fell near Murchison, Victoria, Australia, in 1969. While they did not appear to be of biological origin, they did show that building blocks of life, such as amino acids, can form by chemical means in nature, elsewhere in the universe than on earth.

From studies of moon rocks and meteorites, we are beginning to nail down the birth date of our universe at something like 4.5 billion years ago, and if we are to understand the mysteries of creation and life itself, the knowledge will come from deep space investigations.

There are two schools of thought which explain the origin of the universe in radically different ways. According to the steady state theory (continuous creation), the question of origin has no meaning because the universe has no beginning, no end.

According to another concept, the evolutionary theory, more than 15 thousand million years ago the universe was in its original state—a primeval atom, containing the entire mass of the universe as we know it today—10^{21} tons packed into a volume no bigger than our own solar system, a million million times the density of water.

Beautiful Whirlpool Galaxy—no beginning, no end?

Such a supercondensate would be highly unstable, and must have suffered some radioactive disintegration (the Big Bang theory) that caused the material to spread out through space. Now, after 1,500 million years of time, space occupies 1,500 million light years, and is still expanding.

Says Sir Bernard: "Under the evolutionary theory the future of the cosmos is bleak—the material is dispersing and the universe will die; whereas the continuous creation theory leads to the concept of an infinite future existence, with new galaxies forming as others rush away and vanish."

These are profound ideas, which recall the proud moment when spaceship *Eagle* sat silently at Tranquility Base, on the first manned lunar landing, July 20, 1969, and Astronaut Edwin (Buzz) Aldrin radioed earth:

"Houston, this is Eagle . . . this is the LM pilot speaking. I would like to request a few moments of silence. I would like to invite each person listening in, wherever and whomever he may be, to contemplate for a moment the events of the past few hours, and give thanks in his own individual way."

GLOSSARY

ADVANCED LOGISTIC SYSTEM—A space shuttle providing logistic support to a space station or space base.

APOLLO TELESCOPE MOUNT—A space telescope system designed for use on early Apollo Applications orbiters.

ARTIFICIAL GRAVITY—An accelerative centrifugal force created by a body in rotation.

CENTRIFUGAL FORCE—A force tending to impel an object outward from a center of rotation.

CROSS RANGE MANEUVERS—The lateral flight path of a space shuttle decelerating from orbital to landing speed.

DELTA WING—A triangular-shaped aerospacecraft wing suitable for subsonic, supersonic, and hypersonic flight.

DYNA-SOAR—A proposed Air Force hypersonic boost glide vehicle for unpowered orbital flights.

ELECTROSTATIC PROPULSION—An experimental spacecraft power system using a plasma of electrically charged particles for propulsion.

FREE FLYING MODULE—A space station module which orbits independently of the station itself and can be docked remotely for data retrieval.

G FORCE—A force equal to the earth's gravitational pull at the surface.

HIGH-ENERGY APPROACH—A high-speed, steep approach to landing offering positive control.

HYPERSONIC—A speed five or more times the speed of sound in air.

L/D—The relationship of an airfoil's lift to its drag; the higher the L/D number, the better its efficiency.

LIFTING BODY—A wingless aircraft which obtains lift from the areodynamic shape of its body alone.

MACH NUMBER—The ratio of the velocity of an object to the speed of sound in the vicinity of the object.

MULTIPLE DOCKING ADAPTER—A pressurized space station cell to which more than one shuttle craft or experiment module can be docked.

MULTI-SPECTRAL PHOTOGRAPHY—A means of recording an object's radiations at both visible and invisible wavelengths of the electromagnetic wave spectrum.

NUCLEAR REACTOR—A device to obtain power from the heat of a controlled chain reaction of fissionable material.

ORBITER—That part of a shuttle craft system which goes into orbit to rendezvous with a space station.

REACTION CONTROLS—Small rocket thrusters on an aerospacecraft that change its attitude in space, where aerodynamic flight controls are ineffective.

REENTRY VEHICLE—A spacecraft designed to reenter the earth's atmosphere from outer space.

SATURN WORKSHOP—The manned central core of a Skylab space station, consisting of a modified S-IVB rocket stage.

SOLAR CELL—A device for converting sunlight into electrical energy.

SPACE BASE—An assemblage of space station segments into a larger satellite, where up to 100 scientists can live and work.

SPACE SICKNESS SYNDROME—Symptoms of illness believed caused by living in extended weightlessness or exposure to space radiations.

SPACE STATION—A permanent manned satellite in earth orbit.

SPACE TRANSPORTATION SYSTEM—A system of space shuttles and orbiting space stations by which passengers may travel into space and back economically in reusable craft.

INDEX